BICKL

A Visitor's

You may well have visited the famous Bickleigh Bridge and admired the beautiful riverside scene, something thousands of visitors do each year, but are you aware of the rich and colourful past surrounding this lovely location? Hopefully this little book will give an insight into Bickleigh's history and heritage.

So what do people think of when they hear the name Bickleigh? Some will, of course, think of the 'other' Bickleigh in Devon, on the outskirts of Plymouth. But anyone who lives in or around the Exe Valley will surely conjure up an image, in the mind's eye, of a beautiful place beside the Exe where an ancient stone bridge temporarily slows up traffic in its haste to speed between Exeter and Tiverton. For the most part the village's houses and cottages stand on the valley side, aloof from the traffic that passes below them along the meandering A396 Exe valley road.

All good calendars of Devon scenes should include the view of Bickleigh as seen from the bridge looking up river. It's one of the classic camera shots.

However, the romance of the river is diminished, somewhat, when the translation of Bickleigh's name is attempted because one suggested interpretation is 'a place of cows'. This is not a gem of information usually included in advertising Bickleigh's charms to the outside world!

To many families Bickleigh is a place to go for an enjoyable day out – to the Devonshire's Centre or maybe to the 'castle'. Those who like a rural, rustic ramble, along muddy lanes, or over rolling hills, may even use it as their starting point for a walk as there are numerous strolls that can be enjoyed from here.

Bickleigh, set in a lovely location surrounded by high hills that seem to scrape the sky, is not just an amalgam of pubs and tourist attractions. This literary snapshot of what it was like in the year 1850, when most country villages were more self-sufficient in terms of shops, services and employment, is part of the entry from *White's Directory* of that year.

BICKLEIGH village, on the east bank of the river Exe, 4 miles S. of Tiverton, and 10 miles N. of Exeter, has in its parish 362 souls, and 1835 acres of land, including Chederleigh hamlet. Sir W. P. Carew is lord of the manor, and owner of a great part of the soil; and the rest belongs to

Sir T. D. Acland, Dr. Troyte, and a few smaller proprietors. Bickleigh anciently belonged to a family of its own name, and passed from the Courtenays to a younger branch of the Carews ... Here was buried Major John Gabriel Stedman, who published the History of Surinam, and died in 1797. The Church (St. Mary,) was mostly rebuilt in 1843, at the cost of about £1400. It has a tower and five bells, and contains several neat monuments of the Carew family, one of which has recumbent effigies of a knight and lady. The rectory... is in the patronage of Sir W. P. Carew, and incumbency of the Rev. Robt. B. Carew, M.A., who has a good residence and 60 acres of glebe.

Schooling at Bickleigh, despite the small size of the village, has been continuous since 1826, when the first Day School was supported by the Rector. The National School, built on Glebe land, opened in 1841. It became purely a primary school from 1947 onwards, when its senior pupils were transferred to Tiverton. Following the closure of the school at Cadeleigh, in 1958, the numbers at Bickleigh swelled to the extent that a new school was urgently required, which Bickleigh got in 1960. Today it has an excellent reputation but it has had to endure the wrath of the elements at times.

Although Bickleigh is sheltered beneath high hills there have been moments when the elements, at their wildest, have paid an unwelcome visit. Pat Whatley, a former classroom assistant at the school, came within a few inches of her life when, during a hurricane in 1990, a section of the roof landed on her. She suffered a broken arm, partial memory loss and bruised ribs, but as this was deemed 'an Act of God' compensation wasn't forthcoming!

Today the village centre is generally a quiet place and only a small proportion of visitors explore it. Those who make the effort to walk up the hill will see its lovely thatched cottages but will find a distinct lack of shops. The Old Post Office is now one in name only, trading as a 'Bed & Breakfast' establishment. When the village's bakery closed down in July 1979, it was a sad day for Silverton man Fred Down who had worked there for 26 years. Barry Cave had run this business, in conjunction with being the village postmaster, for some seven years but felt it was uneconomical to continue.

Life, despite appearing to be the same from day to day, has changed. Benjamin Gould was the wheelwright in 1850 and, he having completed his life cycle, another local character was listed in the same skilled profession in 1935. Mr F. Christopher was then at the grand old age of 82 and still turning out wheels. His claim of being the oldest wheelwright in Devon gave him much publicity.

A major fire occurred on 4 June 1998 which destroyed a terrace of four thatched cottages close to the church. The Bond family, who had lived in one of these cottages for six generations, lost antiques and irreplaceable heirlooms despite the great efforts of a large number of fire crews. Fortunately nobody was hurt.

The nearby village green is a small triangular area and bears this award-winning welcome to those who discover it. It won the 1988 'Village Sign Competition' and is the work of V. Wright of Bickleigh who designed and made it.

Since the 1980s *The Bickleigh Bugle*, with a circulation of about 100 copies, has kept folks informed about life and events in and around the village. This much-appreciated local journal appears on the first of each month, except August when the earlier July edition is a 'bumper issue' designed to span the two peak months of high summer. "I'd be lost without it!" is how one villager summed up its importance to the local community.

The village, by nature of its lovely setting and its convenient position, four miles from Tiverton and ten miles from Exeter, has attracted that other creature of habit, the commuter. Many make the daily pilgrimage up or down the valley to work in the larger centres of population. Increased mechanisation has reduced the number of people who derive their livelihoods from the land.

Bickleigh's village hall, a meeting place for many groups, was greatly in need of refurbishment in the mid-1980s and so several fund-raising events were staged. The River Exe became the perfect 'playground' for the 'Bickleigh Belles' who donned Edwardian bathing costumes, mounted a strange craft, resembling a river horse, and were joined by others in a fund-raising splash-about. A street party was also held which generated a real community atmosphere, as almost every household participated in some shape or form.

The famous Bickleigh Bridge takes a daily battering from the volume of traffic that it carries. It was never constructed to carry the loads that it bears today. Built originally as a pack horse bridge, between 1630 and 1640, its engineer was Hiram Arthur. There was a rhyme, uttered by an 87-year-old man in 1790, long after Hiram's death, that placed the responsibility of the bridge's structure and strength firmly at his door.

"If Bickleigh Bridge should chance to stand,
Then Hiram Arthur will be the man.
If Bickleigh Bridge should chance to fall,
Then Hiram Arthur must pay for all."

Throughout the years there have been accidents on the bridge. In Victorian times James Rossiter was riding a young colt that was only partially broken in. When it had carried its rider to the middle of Bickleigh Bridge it suddenly took fright and leapt over the parapet of the bridge. The rider was luckier than the poor horse; he escaped with minor cuts and bruises but the colt suffered a broken neck.

A cold spell of weather in January 1981 led to a spate of accidents around the county. A 48-ton mobile crane slid on ice as it crossed Bickleigh Bridge towards Tiverton. The weight of the vehicle took it through the parapet, leaving it precariously suspended above the fast flowing River Exe. The driver carefully edged his way to the passenger side and made good his escape from an almost certain death in the icy flood waters some feet below. A 25-foot stretch of parapet was demolished and the road blocked for over four hours, but fortunately the driver, from Middlesex, survived without injury.

And it's not just ice that is slippery – the odd 'banana skin' has been known to put the skids under moving objects. In September 1984 a Fyffes lorry skidded, having swerved to avoid a deer. Again the parapet of the bridge was breached, and locals continued their fight for a by-pass. Such a scheme, had it been adopted, would probably have meant the demolition of the old railway station's buildings close to it.

No road accidents, though, as far as we know, have occurred as a result of startling spectral appearances on Bickleigh Bridge.

In late June 1981 the *Express & Echo*, Exeter and East Devon's evening newspaper, carried the following story:

"... Suddenly, though, there it was ... the unmistakable clip-clop of hooves and the shadowy headless rider, in armour, at the end of the village's 400-year-old bridge.

Nineteen-year-old Joanna Cruwys ... of Exeter, was hoping for a glimpse of the ghost of the man her ancestor slew on the bridge in 1332."

This was Sir Alexander Cruwys who, with a sword, ran through a member of Bickleigh's famous Carew family and then threw the body into the downstream side of the Exe.

Ever since that fateful day, so the Bickleigh legend goes, the victim rides across Bickleigh Bridge on June 24. The report continued...

"Last night saw the first, official, Bickleigh ghost watch. Mr Meredith, a county council official in Exeter, organised it all right down to a couple of British Railway red-and-green signalling lamps to stop the traffic at midnight.

Right on time the rider rode ... but the horse turned out to be a pony that made straight for Happy Meadow, the village cricket ground and the man on horseback suddenly dismounted and the armour-bearer made his way towards Bickleigh Castle." The article went on to say that it should suffice to name the 'ghost' as 'Sir Fred of Bickleigh' and the impression is that someone tried to pull a fast one, which is a shame as two hundred eager-to-be-spooked spectators had assembled in the garden of the Fisherman's Cot overlooking (or should it be underlooking?) the bridge. The pub put on refreshments and was a scene of great revelry and high expectation as the time drew towards the anticipated haunted happening. But there was also confusion over the timing of the ghostly guest appearance, for would it be midnight or 1.00 a.m.? Was the knight in BST (British Spectral Time) or GMT (Ghostly Mean Time)? And would any self-respecting spook appear to such a throng? The chances are that if the knight took the night off, if you'll excuse the pun, then he would have made his necessary journey to the bridge at a different time to fulfil his eternal obligation. Those who claim to have seen him on other occasions provide the detail that the victim is much shorter now than he was when a mere mortal. This is because, as a ghost, he is headless and crosses the bridge with his head tucked under his left arm whilst wielding a sword in his right hand. Sir Alexander's attack on a Carew was, apparently, the result

of an argument about a fair lady. What is rather strange about the choice of venue for this apparition is that this particular bridge wasn't there in his time!

His spirit is not the only one here: several spooks haunt the bridge and its environs. Another, this time a ghostly lady, is sometimes seen walking across the river beneath the bridge, just above the weir. This is an experience that locals can only match in times of severe drought when the river runs at a trickle. There were pictures in the press, in September 1933, when Bickleigh villagers were photographed in midstream. In January 1940 the river partly froze over here, but nobody was foolhardy enough to test the thickness of the ice.

The bridge, scheduled as an ancient monument, was featured, albeit briefly, in a survey of Devon, in 1932, commissioned by the Devon Branch of the Council for the Preservation of Rural England. It listed its features as having five arches, two of them round and three segmental. It gave its date as about 1630 and also added that it was reconstructed at a later, unspecified date. It was, according to the report, in a state of good repair.

The Fisherman's Cot was built in the early 1930s at a prime spot on the banks of the Exe and where roads converge. It has its ghosts. Darren Yeates, a young manager, had the job of locking up in the early 1990s, and sometimes, after private functions, this was particularly late. It was only on these occasions, when the bewitching hour of midnight had passed, that he would have a ghostly visitor. Long after the last guest had gone, he would hear a woman's voice talking, "Hello! How are you?" followed by laughing – but there was nobody there. On one occasion he called his pair of chocolate-coloured Labradors, Jake and Harry. When they didn't appear he went to look for them, only to discover that they were crouched down in fear behind a desk in reception. The voice was heard again and both dogs leapt over the three-foot-high desk and bolted out of the hotel door!

The ghostly lady developed a little party trick. Whenever the opportunity arose she would take soft drink bottle tops and throw them around whilst giggling at her own antics.

It has been consistently rumoured that Paul Simon once played, for a modest fee, at the Jolly Porter Folk Club near St David's Station in Exeter. At the time he is supposed to have stayed at or near the Fisherman's Cot for several weeks. The popular belief suggests that he was, on one later occasion, gazing at the sparkling waters flowing beneath Bickleigh Bridge when the inspiration for 'Bridge Over Troubled Water' suddenly came to him. Although the story is probably more liquid than solid in its reliability, it's still a lovely and romantic notion to think that such a classic song may have its roots here in the heart of Devon. However, it is known that the other half of the famous musical duo, Art Garfunkel, stayed at the Fisherman's Cot in 1968, with his brother. He danced with the daughter of the then landlord, Mr Townsend, and signed copies of his records for her.

Mr Townsend, who passed away in 1994, once owned a race horse called 'Fisherman's Cot'. Its golden moment was a victory at Ascot in 1976 when it romped home in the Black & White Whisky Hurdle at odds of 20-1.

One singer that we know definitely was at the Fisherman's Cot for a while was Craig Sullivan. He was known as 'the Singing Landlord' on account of his regular, spontaneous renditions of operatic music. He had had a singing career that had taken in La Scala in Milan and the Welsh National Opera Company. He was no stranger to the Exe valley, having been the landlord at the Three Horseshoes at Cowley Bridge on the outskirts of Exeter, before moving to the Ruffwell near Thorverton, a few miles downstream from Bickleigh Bridge. He was certainly the sort of landlord who could sing for his supper!

Another famous star to entertain visitors with his own rendition of 'Bridge Over Troubled Water' at the pub was David Copperfield, who rose to international fame with Lenny Henry and Tracy Ullman as one of the three members of the 1980s television comedy series *Three of a Kind*. In the mid-1980s he came to Devon on a fishing holiday and liked it so much that he made Bickleigh his permanent home. Since being here he has acquired new skills and has even thatched the roof of his own cottage. The picture was taken when David sang as part of an hour-long special broadcast about Bickleigh, presented by John Govier, for BBC Radio Devon.

The Fisherman's Cot has had a procession of owners. In 1979 Sir Fred Pontin saw it as the ideal purchase to make his retirement more challenging and kept it for several years.

In 1987 it was felt that it was in need of a major face-lift so almost three-quarters of a million pounds was spent on a complete refurbishment. The pub boasted technology rarely seen in such establishments at that time. There was a computer based on the BBC's Domesday project where customers had, at their fingertips, all sorts of historic information that could be called up onto a video screen. On the walls were holograms and also framed collections of toys and models in display cabinets.

Bickleigh, despite its smallness, is blessed in having not one but two fine pubs. The older establishment, the Trout Inn, was originally called the New Inn but is believed to be as old as the current Bickleigh Bridge. In one of the fireplaces is part of an inscribed stone that was removed from the bridge in 1722 when it was enlarged.

Like its licensed neighbour down the road it too has had many owners and shares the same

distinction of being owned by that famous holiday camp entrepreneur Fred Pontin, who bought it in 1984.

The Trout, once complete with petrol pump, is haunted by the ghost of a former chef. Mr Latham, the owner in 1989, saw him soon after taking over the pub. The chef appeared from a cupboard in the kitchen and leant on a sideboard for a while before disappearing. It's not known what prompts this restless soul to haunt the pub.

The pub changed hands, again, in November 1997 and attracted plenty of publicity in the local press because it was bought by one of its regular customers. For Steve Flaws, a Tiverton businessman, it was seen 'as a dream come true'. His 'fairy-tale purchase' was not a complete surprise, because four generations of his family had been in the licensed trade and he became the fifth. However, the pub changed hands once more in the early summer of 1998.

On the opposite side of the ever-busy A396 is the beautiful Bickleigh Cottage, still an attractive guest house, and the subject of many a photograph when viewed from Bickleigh Bridge. There was a delightful entry in Ashley Courtenay's 1938 guide book *Let's Halt Awhile in Devon, Cornwall, and Somerset*

(or as the publisher preferred, for sheer simplicity, "MDCCCCXXXVIII"). For a shilling you could discover that: *"... here is one of the most attractive guest houses in Devon, Bickleigh Cottage. A little sun trap. A floral paradise. Sweet little bedrooms overlooking the laughing waters of the Exe. A little cottage of good food and contentment, where the best is ever for the guests – for Bickleigh Cottage is not open for meals to non-residents. Here the days go all too quickly ... fishing, hunting (three packs), golf at 'Tivvy'* [Tiverton] *... or just watching the Exe tumbling on to the sea."*

The Exe, despite its great beauty and its 'laughing waters', has posed problems to those who live along its banks on a great number of occasions, the floods of October 1960 being some of the most memorable. Much of Devon's lowlands was inundated, great hardship and heartbreak being inflicted on those living in the nether regions. Nevertheless when the main railway line from Taunton to Exeter was impassable, trains still managed to travel the Exe Valley line, even though there were extensive floods at Bickleigh. One of the lighter moments of this inundation occurred when the home of Mr and Mrs Hitt greeted an unusual visitor. A foot-long grayling swam into the kitchen! Mr Hitt told the press that he intended to have it stuffed and placed over the fireplace, thereby continuing the time-honoured tradition of mounting exceptional catches as triumphant trophies.

Since those floody, muddy days of yesteryear much work has been done to tame the Exe of its wettest and wildest ways. Flood alleviation schemes, in several locations, have helped to cope with high volumes of water all frantically trying to get between the piers of Bickleigh Bridge in their rush to return to the sea to complete the water cycle in record time. However, even in recent years there have still been floods that have been spectacular enough to be covered by television companies and to make the front page headlines of the *Express & Echo* yet again! The unfortunate Trout Inn and many other low-lying houses have been flooded to a depth of several feet, and the road to Exeter closed for many hours.

The Exe valley is joined at Bickleigh by another river, the River Dart! But it has nothing to do with its more illustrious Dartmoor namesake and does not originate on that distant moor. It flows from the north-west direction through a deep, steep valley. Having finally flowed under Dart Bridge, close to the Fisherman's Cot, it adds its waters to the Exe a short way below Bickleigh Bridge.

The Chronicles of Twyford (this is the old name for Tiverton) features this account from the early 1860s of an episode that took place on the section of the River Exe between Tivvy and Bickleigh. *"A curious incident took place ... in connection with the Exe, and excited a good deal of interest. A number of tradesmen, assembled as their custom was in the smoking-room of the 'Three Tuns', and were discussing the subject of the River Exe and its depth at different places, when two of the party offered for a wager to go in a boat from Tiverton Bridge to Bickleigh Bridge without landing, or even leaving the boat in those parts of the river where the water was too shallow to float it. Many were the bets made on the event, and the interest felt in the result in-duced a number of the sporting fraternity to betake themselves in the early morning to Bickleigh, where mine host, Roger Upton, of the New Inn* [now The Trout Inn] *had prepared a substantial breakfast. Meanwhile the adventur-*

ous voyagers pursued their way on the river, ever and anon encountering a 'stickle', i.e., a shallow part where the rocky bed had scarcely a foot of water. With infinite toil they propelled their craft by pressing against the rock, making up for lost time when they again reached deeper water. As the time of their anticipated arrival drew near, an excited crowd took up their station on Bickleigh Bridge, eagerly gazing up the river, and betting was more brisk than ever. At length, a little before nine o' clock, a tremendous shout arose as the oarsmen, Mr Bob Pring and his companion, were discovered urging their craft gallantly towards the landing place, opposite the

"New Inn", in time to win the bet with a few minutes to spare. After any amount of handshaking and cheering the whole party sat down in mine Host's great parlour, to partake of a substantial breakfast. The boat was afterwards taken to Tiverton in a waggon, and thus ended one of the strangest voyages ever undertaken by any denizen of old Twyford."

Probably the best book ever written about Devon was Raymond Cattell's *Under Sail Through Red Devon,* first published in 1937. It was republished in two halves in the late 1980s. In the two books Ray travels the coast of Devon in a tiny two-seater boat, having adventures and encounters along the way. He also includes a lot of local history in them. The idea was to explore the coasts and on reaching main rivers sail or canoe up them as far as possible and to explore the surrounding district on foot. This, then, is how he got on at Bickleigh when there seemed a little confusion about where he was. Let the maestro tell you of his and his young German lady companion, Erica Schuppe's, 'close encounter of the third kind' on that fickle summer's day all those years ago…

"Emerging between walls of wooded hills we saw an old stone bridge in the distance. The air, which seemed positively hot, began to drop big spots of rain from turbulent grey clouds, and we spurred our flagging energies in a race for the bridge. We never gained its shelter, for a weir barred the way immediately below it. It was a very simple weir but we could not find the energy to climb it.

Beyond the rippling weir edge, beneath the gentle arches of the bridge we glimpsed a placid pool of water, mirroring in its surface an exquisite stretch of riverside with some sweet thatched cottages and an old inn. The river was beginning again, blossoming afresh in its periodical rebirth.

But it could not tempt us. Our bodies ached as if we, rather than Sandpiper, *had been dragged over all the boulders from Thorverton. 'Enough … Let's leave it till tomorrow.'*

… Stepping ashore we met a bewhiskered ancient, the very image of the one farther back by Thorverton.

'What place would this be?' I asked, rendered nervous by the strange coincidence of the apparition.

'Tees the bridge oover t' river Exe, maister,' he replied.

'My fren' means how you call thees leetle town,' interjected Erica, thinking to improve matters.

'Steady,' I whispered, *'don't confuse him. He's doing his best, in fact he's getting on very well for these parts.'* I cleared my throat and began again.

'The lady's a foreigner,' I explained. *'She meant ...'*

'Du 'er coom vrum Karnwall?' he asked, with new interest. *'My vaather went to Launceston wen 'ee were a bai and 'ee told oy ...'*

'Pardon me,' I interrupted, *'but it's raining hard and I want to know where we are.'*

'Us doan't ca' this yeer rain,' he exclaimed, astonished at my ignorance.

'Perhaps he's dead,' said Erica

'You mean "deaf",' I corrected her. *'Now say something terrific in German, to ease my feelings while I have a brainwave.'*

I had one. *'Would you like a drink?'* I asked.

'Thaat's very koind of 'ee maister. Coom over to t'pub.'

'What's the place called where the pub is?' I asked, quivering ...

His face beamed with understanding. *'Ah, you mean where be 'ee tu?'*

'Yes' I sobbed.

'Us calls un Bickleigh but the railway folks calls un Cadeleigh,' he said, pointing to the little railway halt on which I now saw Cadeleigh plainly written.

'Well', I said, *'they're both nice names. I'll make my mind up later which to call it.'*

At the pub it became clear that Cadeleigh, the village proper, was two miles *'up a grat 'ill and out of sight."*

Ray Cattell later visited this hillside village and several more closer to the fringe of the Exmoor area. What Ray probably didn't know was that when the station was opened it was called 'Cadeleigh & Bickleigh' but from May 1906 it was shortened to just Cadeleigh. This choice was made as the other Bickleigh, nearer to Plymouth, might have caused some confusion to rail travellers.

When Ray Cattell finally left Bickleigh, to experience a decidedly tricky return journey downstream, the innkeeper, the postman, two old women, sundry children and an old mongrel turned up to wave them goodbye.

The second half of the nineteenth century in Devon was a time when the railroad was taken to all the corners of the county. Hardly any village escaped the attention of the railway entrepreneurs who created a network across Devon. Valley routes were always preferred, provided that the menace of any potential flooding river could be considered and counteracted by engineering excellence. This is an extract from the newspaper report of 6 May 1885, recording the opening of the railway between Stoke Canon, where the Exe branch left the main line, and Dulverton.

"After twenty years of anxious waiting the North Devon Railway, along the Exe valley, from Exeter, through Tiverton to Dulverton is at last open throughout and in full working order. The northern section, from Tiverton to Dulverton, was opened about six months ago. The south section ... could not be completed by the same time and it was not ready for inspection until the latter end

of April. Major General Hutchinson, one of Her Majesty's Inspector of Railways, went over the line on the 25th ult., and tested every part of it most carefully with results which were so satisfactory that the opening took place on Friday last – May Day. The length of the line from Tiverton Station to Stoke Canon Junction is 10 3/4 miles and one chain [22 yards]. It reduces the distance by rail between Exeter and Tiverton to 14 3/4 miles. The station buildings comprise, in each case, a covered waiting place open to the line with an inner waiting room at one end for passengers generally and leading out of it a waiting room for ladies. At the other end of the waiting place is the booking office which also serves the purpose of a parcel and general office. Adjoining each station is a house for the stationmaster. The buildings at all four stations are built of Burlescombe limestone with Bath-stone dressings. All the internal woodwork and most of the furniture is of pitch pine and the platforms are paved with glazed blue bricks. The clocks are supplied by Skarratt of Worcester... The stationmaster at Cadeleigh and Bickleigh is Mr J. Smallridge, 2 and a half years at Swimbridge, and winner of the Great Western Railway Company's prize last year for the best-kept station flower garden on the line...

The opening of the line attracted very little notice at Exeter and Tiverton but the residents along the district showed their appreciation of the accommodation provided for them by keeping up 'May Day' somewhat after the good old fashion. The first passenger train which ran the new line left Exeter at 6.30 a.m. and was accompanied to Dulverton and back by Mr J. Campfield, Chief District Traffic Superintendent... The engines on all the trains during the day were neatly decorated with floral garlands and greenery. Very few passengers booked at either terminal nor were many picked up on the way and the total number of persons accommodated by both trains being considerably below a hundred. The stations on route were very tastefully decorated. Later

in the day they were filled with crowds of people who appeared much interested in watching the trains as they came and went to the loud booming of fog signals which had been placed on the line and the shouting and the waving of hats... The principal rejoicings of the event took place at Thorverton... At Bickleigh and Cadeleigh the opening of the line was celebrated with much *heartiness. There was a good display of bunting at the station and in the village a rural fete was successfully carried in a field kindly lent by Mr Merson..."*

When the railway was a new innovation there were those who opposed the visual intrusion into the countryside but Miss Gibbons, of East Budleigh, had few misgivings. She travelled around Devon in 1885 in a donkey cart and wrote of the places that she visited in a much gentler age. This is what she thought of the railway here: *"Even the certainly unpicturesque new object, the new railway, cannot spoil the charm of Bickleigh Bridge and the sight of it reminds one that many people can now visit this most lovely spot who would otherwise have been unable to reach it."*

Ray Cattell also saw the railway in its working days and charmingly described it with these words: *"If you would see the Exe Valley easily the only way is to take that little two-carriage train to Dulverton. You will sit among farmers who will talk for the whole journey about one sheep until, when you see the creature, you gaze at it in amazement, with newly opened eyes, beholding for the first time how much wisdom, poetry, science and drama can be wrapped up in the life of a common sheep. On market days each little station will embark a company of farmers' wives with many baskets, more children and still more conversation, any and all of which encumbrances they will unload on you on the slightest provocation."*

J. M. Slader in *Downalong the Exe* (1966) paints some different, but equally evocative memories from the same era: *" ... Here the railway runs parallel with the road. Suddenly from out of the mists of time, from those clouded days of youth in an unemployed and poverty-stricken Britain of the '30s, there came the vision of a train upon the little single track line, a train which appeared to be overflowing with children; above the steam and the clatter, above the whistle as she sped on through Cadeleigh Station, the hilarious laughter of happy schoolchildren, buckets and spades, candyfloss and toffee-apples. A Sunday school outing to Exmouth. O happy days of the English countryside."*

That train journey up or down the valley was a slow one. It took about half an hour to steam the short distance to Exeter St David's and about ten leisurely, lovely minutes to reach nearby Tiverton.

In 1965, following the closure of the railway, Lord Amory purchased the famous 'Tivvy Bumper', the engine which trundled up and down the Exe valley thousands of times in its working life. Today you can still see this much revered locomotive at the excellent Tiverton Museum.

In 1998 Cadeleigh Station opened as a railway museum to reflect much of the history of Devon's former railways. Those who love engine rides can enjoy a miniature railway journey there and wallow in the glory of those days when there was a decent network of lines covering and crossing the county.

We have already given plenty of space to ghosts and to pubs, but now it's time to move from 'spirits', of various types, to wine! Since 1968 certain south-facing slopes at Bickleigh have been used as a vineyard for the production of some fine English wines. At Yearlstone, high on a spur of land between the Exe and Dart, Gillian Pearkes successfully produced the grapes to fill many a bottle of wine. Indeed when Margaret Thatcher celebrated her tenth year in office as Prime Minister she enjoyed a glass or two of wine that originated here. Yearlstone Vineyard concen-

trates on quality rather than quantity. Gillian was the daughter of the owner of the ancient Yearlstone House which was owned by Redvers, Earl of Devon in the twelfth century. Sadly, Gillian passed away in 1992 and for the following three years the normally sunny slopes 'had a cloud hanging over them' and were out of production. Fortunately Roger and Juliet White reopened the vineyard in 1995 and, having extended the acreage, achieved further success. Perhaps we should raise a glass, or even two, to them!

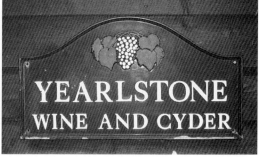

For those wine-buffs, would-be viti-culturalists or just interested folk who make the effort to visit 'Devon's oldest Vineyard', apart from the free tastings they can also 'drink-in' the wonderful, almost intoxicating view straight down the Exe valley from the top of these slopes, where there is also an orchard producing cider apples. On the right day this hillside is the perfect place for a picnic. From this vantage point Bickleigh Bridge can be spied, as can its hillside church. It is also the best viewpoint to appreciate the setting of Bickleigh where two valleys unite, the lesser-known Dart, or Little Dart, also carving out a deep depression as it slyly flows under Dart Bridge and behind the Fisherman's Cot, in its last reaches before joining the Exe.

Although this is an idyllic spot it was the scene, in 1939, of another major fire. This time a cottage called 'Forwards' was gutted. The occupier, Mrs Kelland, was unaware that the thatched roof was on fire but a passing lorry driver, from Exeter, saw the flames and alerted the widow. Helpers managed to remove much of the furniture but the blaze raged for three hours and the property was destroyed. However, like the phoenix from the ashes, it was later rebuilt.

An extremely popular local television series, of recent years, has been David Young's *Cobblestones, Cottages & Castles*. In the closing sequences of each programme of the first two series, the presenter was seen with his faithful Labrador, Oliver, strolling along a stretch of road as the credits rolled. He has been asked literally thousands of times where this was filmed. The answer is, along the lane that runs from Bickleigh Bridge to Bickleigh Castle. If you happen to walk along there and get that sense of *déjà-vu*, then this might just explain it.

Bickleigh Castle (shown as Bickleigh Court on 1906 maps) is now partly a tourist attraction, 'Where history comes to life…', and has also been featured in David Young's programmes. Although it doesn't fall into that category of having a striking, dramatic location on a craggy outcrop, it does, nevertheless, have a strength and stoutness about it. It was more of a fortified manor house than a dedicated castle even though it bore many of the features normally found in a castle.

The Courtenays have long held the title of Earl of Devon, their ancestral home today being Powderham Castle beside the Exe Estuary, many miles downstream. About 1390 Bickleigh became one of their many properties, as an estate usually for younger sons. Here they developed an earlier Norman settlement owned previously and at different times by 'Alward the Englishman', the de Bickleighs (Bichelie), William de Balfago and the Pointingtons.

All went well until one Courtenay son died leaving an orphan daughter called Elizabeth. The Courtenays, whose principal residence was at Tiverton until 1539, invited the Carews, their cousins, to take charge and bring up the young girl. But the Bickleigh air was charged with romance, the young Courtenay girl losing her heart to Thomas Carew. The family were less than pleased by this and furious, no doubt, when the starry-eyed lovers ran away together. But Thomas redeemed himself by his brave deeds at the Battle of Flodden in 1513, when he saved the life of Lord Howard, and the Courtenays generously gifted Bickleigh Castle to Elizabeth as a belated wedding present. From there on in and over the following couple of centuries the Carews developed the site into something of a fortress.

Another member of the family, Vice-Admiral Sir George Carew, was the commander of the *Mary Rose* and perished with the rest of the ship's company, so those who take in the exhibition material are in for a real history lesson here.

General Fairfax successfully attacked the castle, defended by Sir Henry Carew, during the English Civil War. He then duly demolished the fortified wings on either side of the inner courtyard and inflicted damage on the impressive gatehouse. Only this and the thatched chapel survived in any salvageable state. As a consequence a cob and thatch farmhouse replaced the earlier fortified house.

Sir Henry's grief was compounded some years later when his only son and his nephew died on the same day. This left him in the sorry situation of not having an heir to inherit his estate. It has been said that his death in 1681 was attributed to a broken heart.

It has seen its moments of high drama but now the only invasion is the gentler one of tourists. It's open to the public in the season with plenty to see including a nun with bullet holes! Fortunately this is only a painting, civil war troops billeted there having used it for target practice. There are also artifacts from that period of English history, among them a helmet and breastplate of a Roundhead soldier.

The Gatehouse dates back to the fourteenth century, when the Courtenays rebuilt on the medieval foundations. The largest room in the castle is the Great Hall, complete with minstrel's gallery, built over the Gatehouse Arch.

But this is by no means the oldest building, because the chapel dates back to somewhere between 1090 and 1110. Much of the masonry is original, the roof probably one that has always been thatched. In the early part of the twentieth century it became derelict and was reduced to the

status of cattle byre for a while before being restored. It is believed to be the oldest complete building in Devon.

One of the castle's striking features is the artistically decorated overmantel of one of the fireplaces. It depicts scenes from The Western or Prayer Book Rebellion of 1549, when a significant number of people were so upset at plans to a have a new English version of the Prayer Book instead of the existing Latin version. Normally quiet rural retreats were awoken from their slumbers by a degree of militancy not normally seen in these parts. The stirrings of discontent rumbled into action at Sampford Courtenay, to the west. After many notable encounters the rebels were eventually suppressed, Sir Peter Carew being instrumental in quelling the cause.

For his efforts the overmantel was presented to him.

The Carews' estate was sold off in 1922, thereby ending a long association with this glorious heart of Devon.

A relaxation of the laws of where weddings may be conducted has meant that the romantic Bickleigh Castle, since the summer of 1997, has also become a favourite venue 'for tying the knot'. The castle can be hired for conferences, concerts and a wide range of other uses.

The church at Bickleigh is de-

scribed by the late Professor Hoskins as being: *"... a badly restored fourteenth century building, with a twelfth century South doorway and font. It is chiefly notable for the charming, though crudely executed, Carew monuments of sixteenth to seventeenth century date."* It is a quiet, serene place surrounded, here and there, by attractive thatched cottages, a world away from the tourist and visitor part of Bickleigh.

There are certain names in Devon that are associated with families of great distinction and a fair number of them begin with C: for example Courtenays, Chichesters, Cliffords, Champernownes and Carews. Two of these have, as we have seen, had strong connections with Bickleigh.

Although they are greatly respected families, occasionally a black sheep has appeared to taint or tarnish the family name. Such is the case with the Carews. Bampfylde Moore Carew was an amazing man, by any yardstick. Should you begin to doubt it then it may be worth tracking down *The Surprising Adventures of Bampfylde Moore Carew* which, on its title page, tells us it contains his life story "*and many entertaining particulars of that extraordinary Man*". It was published in April 1812 and printed for W. Salter of Tiverton and sold by "*Crosby's & Co of London and by booksellers in Exeter, Taunton, Sherborne, Frome, Salisbury, Plymouth & Dock.*" The latter is now Devonport, a place this amazing character would, no doubt, have passed through in one of his many guises. Carew was the ultimate con man. People wise to his various ruses regarded him as a genius, a master of his trade.

He was born in July 1690, his baptism attended by many dignitaries of the day. His father, the Rev. Theodore Carew, Rector of Bickleigh, performed the ceremony.

At the age of twelve he was sent to Blundell's School at nearby Tiverton and here mixed with 'Young Gentlemen of the First Rank'.

However, having got into trouble he ran away from school, thereby signalling the start of an almost unbelievable existence. Using his wits and his skills of disguise and impersonation he later conned people all over the world, to earn the title 'King of the Beggars'. He obtained money, goods or food whilst posing in a vast number of guises, from Quaker minister to shipwrecked sailor. Inevitably he got into many scrapes but led something of a charmed existence before finally 'retiring' back to Bickleigh. His autobiography was called *An Apology for the Life of Mr Bampfylde-Moore Carew* and was written in 1753, five years before he died. His last years were spent at Bickleigh in quiet contemplation following a windfall from an eighteenth century lottery. Lucky beggar!

Devonshire's Centre is another tourist attraction with much to offer the visitor. It was opened by Clive Gunnell as Bickleigh Mill Craft Centre on 26 May 1973. The opening was unusual in that it was screened live on regional television. The present Mill building, mainly constructed of stone, probably dates from early Victorian times but almost certainly lies on the same site as the original mill mentioned in the Domesday book.

The idea for the centre was the brainchild of Bill Shields, who had been a resident in Bickleigh since 1965, and owes much to the experience he gained in multiple and department store retailing around the world.

Until the 1950s it had been a corn mill, but disaster struck when the weir broke and the two mill wheels ground to a halt. The building fell into disuse and all the machinery was removed. For a while part was used for the construction of window frames by a joinery works until it was acquired by Mr Shields in 1971 when, after planning permission was granted, a full restoration programme was embarked upon. The character of the main building was brought back to its original form, whilst the weir was mended and the mill leat (last cleaned by prisoners of war) was fully dredged and the sluice gates repaired.

By coincidence, another Mill, Town Mills in the centre of Dulverton, had closed and been purchased by the town council, who were anxious to clear out most of the working machinery. This, together with the waterwheel (made by Stenners of Tiverton in the last century), was transported down the Exe valley, where it was adapted and reinstated in Bickleigh Mill and may be seen working today.

According to Mr Shields, the programme was like putting 'Humpty Dumpty together again', with his bank balance suffering immeasurably. However, Bickleigh Mill has become Devon's most famous working water mill, with its revered pottery and workshops. It also has an enviable reputation for selling an extensive variety of good-quality merchandise ranging from fudge to fancy goods and from clothing to cuckoo clocks, all displayed on three floors of the building.

In 1974 the adjoining Miller's House was tastefully converted to a restaurant which overlooks the waterwheel. It is now equally well known for its home-made produce and cream teas. For those who like to try their hand at catching Rainbow Trout (and what child doesn't?) the opportunity is available at the Mills Fishing Centre, where equipment and tuition are ready to hand within the main summer season. It all forms part of an intriguing and enjoyable visit to Devonshire's Centre. Keep a lookout for the magnificent free-flying macaws.

For those who want a pleasant stroll from Bickleigh, it is possible to walk up the Exe valley all the way to Tiverton. The route follows the wooded south-east side of the river. It is an attractive walk, particularly when the sunshine illuminates this side of the valley in the afternoon.

And so we have been through fire, floods and 'troubled waters', and met ghosties and ghoulies, villains and victims, kings and killers, singers and songwriters, con men and comedians, and railways and rustics. Who would believe such a beautiful spot should have so many amazing tales to tell?